A STEP OUT
OF
DARKNESS

**How To Help Someone Enter
Addiction Treatment and Walk
With Them Through Recovery**

Joseph B. Devlin

ISBN: 9781795162456

Author Photograph by Michael Cordano

Contents

1
Introduction

"Remember that when you leave this earth,
you can take with you nothing that you have
received--only what you have given: a full
heart, enriched by honest service, love,
sacrifice and courage."
--St. Francis of Assisi

Day after day, night after night I work with,
speak to or bump into at least one person suffering
from addiction. Witnessing their struggles breaks my
heart. I see it in their faces, I hear it in the way they
speak, and I can feel it in my bones. Not only do I see
the person who is being tormented by addiction, I see
the many sons and daughters, mothers and fathers,
grandfathers and grandmothers, aunts and uncles,
friends and co-workers who are devastated, believing
there is no way out. Having been around addiction for
so many years, I know it is sometimes easy to
overlook someone who is struggling with this disease.
For all the people that I see, I know there are millions
more who go unnoticed.

In the United States every eight minutes, a person dies from an overdose. Opioids are killing more people per year than those who were dying at the peak of the AIDS epidemic. Studies show that in 2015, there were enough opioid prescriptions written in America to keep every single American intoxicated 24 hours a day for 3 straight weeks! If you have not been directly impacted by the opioid crisis, you most certainly know of someone who has.

This book is not about blaming, it is about truths. We cannot address this epidemic by ignoring or simply throwing money indiscriminately at it. We as a community need to help one another. Throughout my 20 years in the treatment industry, I have accumulated significant resources and have learned to navigate the system of what we call treatment. I have seen too many families get taken advantage of in the system, and I have seen others take advantage of the system. I want to let people know there is a way out of this addiction quagmire, and this book will help you navigate this process.

Most people do not think there is a way out, and I am here to tell you that I have seen and helped countless individuals and families recover from this hopeless state of mind and body.

My hope is this book will show you what seems to be a complicated process is simpler then you think. You will make hard decisions, but the overall process of entering treatment and what to do after treatment is relatively simple. The hard part is going to be asking for and accepting help. I am here to tell you that the help is here. You no longer have to be confused by what a treatment center is doing while your loved one is there.

I thank you for picking up this book and reading it, and if you have any questions my contact information is in chapter eleven.

May this book help bring peace and grace to you and your family.

Peace Be With You,

Joe

2
National Emergency

"For I know the plans I have for you,
declares the Lord, plans to prosper
you and not to harm you, plans
to give you hope and a future."
--Jeremiah 29:11

There is no shortage of individuals reminding you that we are currently in the midst of an epidemic. The Government recently agreed to put one billion dollars in the federal budget to combat the opioid epidemic and the President just announced, "The opioid crisis is a national emergency." Addiction affects the lives of tens of millions of Americans. Statistics show one in three Americans is affected by the disease of addiction and only 10 percent of those afflicted receive any form of treatment. Simply, if you are not suffering from addiction yourself, you almost certainly know someone who is.

You may be reading this book because you are a professional and want to learn more about how to help someone get into treatment or you may be someone who is trying to get a loved one into treatment. I know you are aware that this epidemic is devastating and shredding the fabric of our society, however, I believe it is necessary to examine a few points.

Addiction has reached a height of epic proportion. It is more common for a person to die from a drug overdose than from a car crash. Addictions are not isolated in one sector of the population. They touch all races, nationalities, economic situations, political lines and family ties. I know that either you or someone close to you will be impacted by addiction. If someone you care about is struggling with an addiction, take action now, as you may not have the option to later.

There are many myths and opinions that surround the causes and conditions of addiction. No matter what your philosophy of why addiction exists, it's extremely prevalent and is devastating our society. This epidemic is not going to disappear very soon or by itself. By all projections, it is only going to get worse. Addiction destroys family relationships, legal systems, finances, people's spirit, and deep meaningful relationships, in effect ripping the very fabric of society.

Knowing what I know, I can no longer sit quiet. I want to share my years of experience and knowledge related to the challenging, confusing, and sometimes overwhelming process of getting a loved one into treatment. I am on this journey with you and we need to plant our flag and solve this problem. One small step, act of love, act of random kindness to help improve an individual's situation may be all that it takes to facilitate the paradigm shift needed to help someone enter the world of recovery.

The overall impact of addiction is overwhelming. In 2015, more than 27 million people in the United States reported current use of illicit drugs or misuse of prescription drugs and more than 66 million people (nearly a quarter of the adult and adolescent population) reported binge drinking in the past month. It is estimated that the yearly economic impact of substance misuse is $249 billion for alcohol misuse and $193 billion for illicit drug use. These staggering statistics leave many people hopeless.

The bottom-line questions are, "Where do we start? What can we do?"

We start by loving the person in front of us. As you will see in this book, our traditional idea of love will take on forms that we may not be used to.

I write this book because people in addiction seem to know more about how to get into treatment than those trying to help them. Many times, this allows them to manipulate a system or the loved ones attempting to help them. After reading this book, you will be on an even playing field with the professional, your loved one and anyone supporting your loved one through treatment. Since the opioid epidemic is what is ravaging our society, I am going to refer often to drugs (heroin especially); however, the information I am presenting to you can be applied to any addiction.

I have worked with countless family members

I have worked with countless family members wondering why their loved one will not just stop using. Why do they chose the substance over their family, children, work, etc.? The common answer I hear from the family member is that their loved one just has a lack of willpower. Unfortunately, this is not the case. People who draw this conclusion draw it in the context of their own situation. If a person does not suffer from a substance abuse problem, they likely do not understand why one cannot just stop.

"Just stopping" is not how recovery actually works. Yes, an addict must stop ingesting the substance; however, active addiction takes over basic primitive instincts. The primitive life instincts and survival skills to eat, protect, and reproduce are overtaken by the need to feed the addiction.

As this occurs, the individual no longer is able to fight the battle about willpower, rationality or the need to do the thing that's right. Neurobiological changes have occurred in the reward circuitry of the brain. The addict's organ and chemical makeup has now changed and the instinct of priority is to feed their addiction. This biological understanding of addiction classifies it as a disease and allows insurance agencies to pay for the treatment. Insurance would not pay for treatment if it were a moral or willpower issue. Let us agree on this biomedical concept before moving forward, focusing on the necessity of treatment rather than attempting to shame an addict into sobriety.

Maybe you do not agree with what I laid out or with what the insurance companies agreed to. Well, let's just say that you are the one who is right. Do you still face the problem of helping a loved one who is in addiction? Are they continuing to use despite negative consequences? Is this the problem at hand? Has nothing so far worked for a successful change? You may now be willing to give treatment a try this time. If so, let's take the next step.

Why do we treat people with addictions in an undignified manner? We would not treat a diabetic by trying to shame them or by telling them to "just stop." We can't do the same thing with addictions. We've tried in the past to do this and failed. There's a history of archaic methods that attempted to solve the addiction problem and they were unsuccessful. We've tried locking people up and instead of helping them, we have institutionalized them. This leaves us trying to find the most useful way to help the addicted loved one.

Behind every addict is a family.

Another characteristic of the addict is that they have resigned themselves to being an addict. They do not want to be an addict the rest of their life but they see no other way out. We can help provide them this lifeline.

Treatment will consist of addressing genetics and environmental factors that attribute to addiction. Treatment will give them hope that they can change their life and stop the addiction. Change will occur on a mental, physical, emotional, behavioral and spiritual level. This holistic approach will allow a person to see and experience how slight changes in every one of these areas can help overcome this hopeless state of mind and body caused by addiction.

There will be a need for a willingness to listen in treatment but not necessarily a willingness to change. To change, an individual will need the help of members of the community. Yes, there are many cases of individuals who were forced to start their recovery due to incarceration, placement into a treatment center or mandated 12-step meetings who were able to change.

There is no one-size-fits-all method for recovery.

A tailored approach for each person is important; however, the solution must address mental, emotional, physical, behavioral and spiritual aspects of life. Addiction has changed many of these core aspects of life for the individual and it only makes sense that these things will need to be addressed for long lasting positive change in the individual's life and family system. Even though the chances of recovery seem bleak right now, let me assure you that recovery has happened for millions of people. Communities will support a loved one and cause change, if you let the communities help.

3
Intervention

"Death and Life are in the power
of the tongue, and those who love
it will eat its fruit."
--Proverbs 18:21

I know you are in the middle of a crisis and need to get your loved one into treatment so I am going to jump a couple steps to outline the most critical part of helping a loved one enter treatment--an intervention. We are going to look at an intervention from the point of view that family members often don't recognize the power of their relationship to influence their addicted loved one. Your suffering loved one is miserable and truly wants to be happy, and I want you to be able to see the impact you can have on this situation.

People often ask, "What is the one common trait happy people share?" The answer according to Harvard's Grant and Glueck 75-year-plus longitudinal study is: They are in quality relationships. It makes sense that people are happier in encouraging relationships, where they have regular contact with and accountability to one another. As social beings, humans want to be in relationships where they are loved and cherished. Consequently, we have more influence to guide our loved one to enter treatment than perhaps we originally thought. This knowledge provides the foundation of a successful intervention.

If you have already had a successful intervention, skip to the next chapter to read how to engage with your insurance provider and continue walking with your loved one through treatment. For those of you who have not had a successful intervention, please continue to read this chapter.

People avoid holding an intervention because they think it indicates they are turning their backs on their loved ones. As you will see, that is the farthest thing from the truth.

You have reached a point where you do not know what to do as nothing has worked. Your loved one will not listen to you. You have faith that your loved one wants a different life and you are tired of watching them kill themselves. Over and over, they have said to you that "this is the time" only for you to find them using again. Everyone else has said, "They're weak... they don't care...you have to give up..."-- yet you refuse.

For your persistence, I offer this plan of action. Find a qualified professional to facilitate an intervention. Many addiction specialists and treatment centers offer intervention services as part of the cost of treatment or for a nominal fee.

Among the reasons to employ a trained professional to conduct an intervention:

- The interventionist can take some pressure off you as frustration and anger will now be diverted to the interventionist.

- The interventionist will help you prepare what to say and how to avoid pitfalls.

- The interventionist facilitates the intervention, putting out any fires and making sure the discussion runs in a timely manner

Often well-meaning adults envision an intervention as trying to convince loved ones to stop their addiction and start treatment by emphasizing all the negative situations they have caused or are enmeshed in. Although this may *feel* right, your loved one already knows the damage they have inflicted, and want to stop--but the addiction completely dominates their life.

So, contrary to what seems right, an intervention is when you want to tell the addict all the things that you love about them. Your interventionist will be able to work with you, so you can say what you want to say, using positive language, such as I statements. (When we are emotionally charged, it is difficult to say what we feel and we often end up expressing an idea that is the exact opposite of what we want to communicate.)

You will speak with the interventionist at least once before you have the intervention. During this meeting, you will discuss what to say, how to say it, and determine a place and length of time for the intervention, including a cutoff point should your loved one refuse treatment.

The intervention does not need to be long. Nor should it be. This is straightforward communication with simple heartfelt words from the mouths of people who love the addict and can no longer stand around and watch them die. But if they choose life, they are willing to walk a million miles alongside and support them.

I have been a part of interventions where after just one loved one shares their support, the addict said, "O.K., I'll go to treatment." Other family members wanted to share what they had prepared and the professional was able to step in and say, "Yes, you can share your support at a later date but right now we need to move forward and get to the treatment center."

This did not go over so well as the family member had put time and effort into preparing what they were going to say and wanted to have their moment to share their thoughts and feelings. Without the trained professional, the situation could have gotten messy. There was no reason to continue the intervention. One of the main objectives of the intervention is to have the addict go to treatment. The addict agreed to go. This is where we stop and take them to the treatment center.

The trained professional will help you keep to your talking points, stay on track and help you get your loved one into treatment. Your addicted loved one will do anything to keep the addiction going and I've seen them tug on the hearts of people and play on past family relationships and dynamics. Although they may be speaking some truth, the addict is dying. Once they put down their substances they will be able to begin to process past relationships and work towards healing. If they don't put down the substance then the healing will not occur.

I remember one intervention I facilitated. There were more than seven loved ones who wanted to participate and express their encouragement and support for the individual. The addict attempted to debate each one of their supporters but as difficult as it was, with the facilitator's prompting, when one person was finished the next one started.

The participants kept to their boundaries and spoke encouragingly while insisting on accountability. I could see how painful it was for each of the loved ones to go through this and not engage in the banter however the addict realized that *this time* was different and they were not going to talk themselves out of this. The addict gave a valiant effort and tried to keep this going as long as they could. They even pulled out their ace card and talked about the death of a parent they never got over and we acknowledged the pain but we let the rest of the surviving family members continue to express their support and love. The addict then increased their dramatics by running outside and their mother said "if you leave you have made your choice." With myself, one other sibling and the addict standing there in the driveway, it only took a few seconds to see the addict come to a moment of clarity. They realized that they needed to go to treatment because the family was standing in solidarity. In a matter of hours, we were able to get the addict into treatment and the family is doing much better today.

This I know: The family system must confront in loving unity and you will have a successful intervention.

As you can see, utilizing a professional for your intervention helps facilitate the process smoothly. Your addicted loved one has been manipulating and tugging on your emotional strings for so long that it can be very hard for you *not* to respond to the manipulation.

When it has come to the end of the intervention here is the hard line. If they're not willing to enter treatment then you can help them find a homeless shelter or they could be escorted to wherever they live. If you do that, make sure there are at least two people with them. A single person may be vulnerable to their attempts at manipulation.

Every family member must stand together in loving unity. From this point on, you are not paying their bills for them anymore. You're not going to do their laundry anymore. You are not going to be cooking their meals anymore. If they choose life, you will lock arms with them and help them walk through every adversity.

You are now ready to have an intervention! Great. Prior to the intervention, it's important to have answers to the following questions:

1. Determine what level of care your loved one needs.

2. Understand your insurance benefits. (see Appendix D for questions to ask insurer)

3. Choose the appropriate treatment center for your loved one to go to.

4. Decide who will facilitate your intervention.

To help you with these decisions, continue reading through this book. You will learn about insurance and ways you can walk with the addicted loved one through the intake process and throughout treatment. Your intervention can happen as quickly or slowly as you would like--I'm here to say let's have it today!

Remember, according to the Grant and Glueck study, the number one common denominator with people who are happy is that they are in positive relationships. We all want to be happy. When we appropriately set boundaries and say to our addict that they need to enter treatment because they matter and we can no longer watch them die, the chance is extremely high that they will choose life. We are all searching for quality relationships that provide fulfillment and happiness. The good life is built on good relationships. This journey of helping your loved one into treatment will help you re-establish this fulfilling relationship with them and allow you to create healthy relationships with people you will meet during this process.

4
Treatment Options

"Two men looked out from prison bars. One saw the mud, the other saw the stars."
-- Dale Carnegie

In this chapter, we will discuss levels of treatment. Let's say that our loved one is in need of an inpatient treatment facility.

I would like to remind you that your loved one's entry into an inpatient treatment facility does not mean that they are "cured." The goal of therapy during a 30-60-90 day rehab program is to prepare an individual in recovery for life after intensive treatment. Therefore, many individuals require continued therapy for many months or years after rehab.

With that said, I want to give you an idea of what treatment may look like. Let us take the all too common example of a loved one who needs to enter an inpatient detox unit. The best course of long term treatment in the ideal world would be a Detox stay (7 days), a step down to Inpatient rehab (28 days), a step down to a Partial Hospitalization Program (PHP) (6 weeks), a step down to an Intensive Outpatient

Program (IOP) (8 weeks), and a step down to General Outpatient (GOP) (continue at least 6 months).

The above is in an ideal world treatment scenario. This is not meant to be a cookie-cutter approach, I just really want you to understand that treatment is not a quick fix. It is not a one and done. I understand the realistic obstacles to committing to this ideal world length of treatment. The two major concerns expressed about this level of commitment are that your loved one will point out the financial difficulty (a legitimate concern) and time constraints. (I would want to know how much time they spent using and compare it to the amount of time they are being asked to be in treatment.) The good news is that they do not have to make a long-term commitment up front. They are not taking on a mortgage but they may be mortgaging their future.

INPATIENT

Detox

Let us begin to review the levels of treatment. Detox is the most common mainstream approach to addiction treatment. Detox is for people who are in active addiction and are experiencing or are going to experience withdrawal. People in active addiction will experience physical withdrawal from their substance of use. (Please see Appendix C.) While there is no doubt they will also experience mental withdrawal from their substance, mental withdrawal alone would not necessarily qualify them to enter a detox unit. For example, if someone were using cocaine and no other substances, they would be admitted to an inpatient unit, but not a detox unit.

In a detox experience, the medical staff and counselors are available to help patients safely go through the detox process. Although detox is a vital component of treatment because it helps patients handle withdrawal and ease cravings, it does little to address the factors that led to drug abuse in the first place.

Detox exists to safely monitor a patient, sometimes providing medication to somebody to lessen the pain of their withdrawal. The epidemic of heroin addiction has greatly increased the administering of medications to help with the withdrawal symptoms. It should be noted that some of the medications being provided to help with withdrawal can be addictive and many times may be one of the substances the addict has been abusing. Some of these medications are in the classification of the opioid and benzodiazepine family. Please ask your facility if your loved one will be receiving medications, how the medications will be used in treatment and any known side effects. You can plan on a typical medically monitored detox stay to last for three to five days and it can last as long as two weeks in extreme cases involving medical conditions and benzodiazepines.

Inpatient

Inpatient treatment may last 30 days but insurance will typically fund for about two weeks. This is not enough time to get everything back on track. While in inpatient rehab, a patient's environment becomes more structured. From the time they wake up in the morning until the time they go to bed at night their day is mapped out. Individuals are assigned a primary counselor (whom they should meet with at least twice a week) and attend scheduled groups throughout the day.

Normal inpatient stays used to be a straight 28 days. Today, most insurance providers will only cover about two to three weeks of inpatient treatment. During this time, the individual's thought process may become less cloudy, and they may learn to follow treatment center rules, develop a "normal" routine for waking up and going to sleep, learn about treatment and addiction and set treatment goals.

During their stay in inpatient treatment, I recommend you have at least one family session a week. These family sessions are in addition to the family session you should have upon their discharge from inpatient treatment. These sessions will allow you to review the treatment plan goals and see what they're working on. A good tool to evaluate your loved one's mindset is to evaluate their treatment goals.

OUTPATIENT

Partial Hospitalization Program (PHP)

Upon completion of inpatient treatment, a person should step down to a Partial Hospitalization Program (PHP) or sometimes referred to as Partial Care. This is a five day a week outpatient treatment, normally scheduled from 9 AM to 3 PM. It has slightly less structure than inpatient treatment and at the end of each day, the individual has the benefit of returning home to live life in their community. Your loved one will meet individually with their counselors a minimum of twice a week and again I suggest attending a family session a minimum of once a month.

Intensive Outpatient Program (IOP)

Rarely an individual will complete an inpatient treatment program and step down to an IOP. A typical IOP has group sessions three days or nights a week with one individual/family session per week. Total time for IOP is a minimum of nine hours a week. I continue to recommend attending a family session a minimum of once a month.

General Outpatient (GOP)

GOP should consist of one group session and one individual/family session a week. Over time the individual will stop attending the group and continue to engage in an individual/family session per week. Follow through is key. Just as with any other treatments, please remember to schedule follow-up appointments. You have invested a lot of time in your loved one's treatment and want to capitalize on the momentum.

The number one misconception about drug and alcohol treatment is that the addict becomes cured. Would a cancer or diabetes patient not have a follow-up appointment? Even if you agree to a six-month checkup, I believe this can only help set you on the path of successful long-term recovery.

One of the main reasons why I see relapse occur is that after someone completes a level of treatment they stop engaging with their support networks or treatment, thus, causing them to lose accountability and connectedness after the treatment. This is one of the reasons AA is so helpful. AA/NA maintains a level of connectedness, follow up, and accountability.

A common reason for resistance to treatment you will hear from someone in addiction is that they don't want to go to treatment because everyone else in there is an addict and they are not one of them. In very few instances this is an actual legitimate concern. The addict wants to stay different. They want to separate and say, "I am better than that person." Who can blame the individual? Our society has trained us to compare ourselves to one another; who has what, and who is most successful. For our current concerns, those who are most successful will be the ones who stay sober.

I have only provided a brief overview of the levels of treatment. My goal was to give you basic insight into the most common levels of services so that you could be familiar with them when you take your loved one in for an evaluation. There are longer term treatment programs that can last 18 months. There are also sober living facilities and medically managed communities just to name a few. You can explore these different levels of services with your counselor as your loved one is in treatment. Which level is right for you? This leads us into our next chapter where we will discuss walking with someone through the intake process.

5
Confidence During Intake Process

"You may not control all the events that
happen to you, but you can decide
not to be reduced by them."
--Maya Angelou

You and your loved one have come to an agreement, made a decision and arrived at this point of time to go to treatment. This is HUGE! You believe you know which level of treatment your loved one should go to, now what? Step one, you need to figure out where insurance will pay for treatment. In this chapter, we are going to talk about the process of admission into treatment.

Many treatment facilities use the terms intake, assessment, and evaluation in different context. At some point your loved one has to have an assessment so that they can have an evaluation acceptable to the insurance company. My goal is to help you get through the red tape and have your loved one successfully admitted into a treatment facility. To help you navigate the red tape, I am going to use the words intake/assessment in this chapter to describe the process that gets you the evaluation needed by the insurer. When beginning the plan of action outlined below, I suggest you grab a pen and notebook and keep notes/journal because the amount of information can get overwhelming.

If you have insurance...

The one thing that needs to be determined right away is what type of insurance you have. This is going to drive where they go to treatment and how long they can stay. The first thing to do is to call the number on the back of your insurance card and find out where the insurance company contracts for drug and alcohol treatment. You should talk with the insurer about the costs of your in-network and out-of-network benefits. Most of the time, your in-network benefits will be less out of pocket for you up front however it limits where treatment can be provided. Your out-of-network benefits will increase the number of possible facilities and if the deductible has been met for the year, then it may be the same cost as going to an in-network provider.

After contacting your insurance company, the next step is to call the treatment facility to find out what their process is for entering their treatment facility. During this contact, you will also find out if there is any availability/openings at this time. Most likely, you will schedule a time to come in for an intake/assessment appointment with your loved one. As long as there is availability and your loved one meets criteria for placement, you will be offered the opportunity to enter the treatment center that day.

Since your loved one may enter treatment that day it is a good idea for them to go to the assessment not under the influence, as impairment may cause a problem. A friend of mine trying to get into treatment begged to have a quart of beer to steady his nerves. After drinking the beer, he showed up for the assessment and was not admitted because he was intoxicated and it was determined that he was not of sound mind to sign himself into a treatment facility.

If your loved one is trying to convince you to get one more "load" in before the assessment or going into treatment, you now have a real-life example as to why they should not do this. The individual needs to sign himself into the drug and alcohol treatment facility. Age does not matter. Yes, even if under the age of 18, the individual must personally sign in. A guardian or parent cannot do this.

There is an exception to the above statement in the law known as ACT 53 in the state of Pennsylvania. ACT 53 allows a parent/legal guardian to get a drug and alcohol assessment for their child, ages 12-17, and if warranted, compel the child to enter treatment; however, this is a process that may hold legal ramifications for the adolescent and is used in rare and extreme cases. If you would like further information on this law, please feel free to contact me.

Side note: I encourage you to always be in contact with the treatment facility and the insurance agent. This way you will know what is being covered and what is not. Also, if the insurance does deny a level of care that you feel your loved one needs, there is an appeal process you can go through. You would need to contact your insurance company regarding this process and the treatment center will be more than willing to help walk you through this appeals process.

If you do not have insurance

If you do not have insurance, the first thing you need to do is contact your county drug and alcohol office. Each county in the state of Pennsylvania has an agency called a Single County Authority or SCA. A simple Google search of the county that you live in will get you the telephone number or you can dial 211 and be connected to an operator who will provide you with contact information for any community service organization that you would like to speak to. You want to call the SCA because you need to find out where they do their assessments (just as with private insurances). Unlike private insurance, your assessment may not occur at the facility you end up being admitted to.

Once you find out where the assessments are done you need to contact that assessment agency. The agency will provide you with information on what you need to take to the assessment.

Today, most assessment sites do not actually schedule time slots for the intake/assessment. Assessments are given on a first come, first served basis. My suggestion is to arrive at least 15 minutes before the assessment site opens to make sure your loved one is seen that day, thus improving their chances of entering treatment that same day.

One of the functions of the SCA is to be a good steward of the county's resources. If you have a job and refused insurance through your employer, the SCA may not agree to fund your treatment.

If you have insurance and declined drug and alcohol coverage as part of your policy, the SCA may choose not to fund your treatment. I would check with your SCA and speak with them about certain situations that may rule you out of the funding pool.

Counties in Pennsylvania cannot currently rule out funding for individuals who are considered to be in a priority population. These priority populations include pregnant women, adolescents, veterans, overdose survivors and injection drug users.

Also, if your loved one is someone who falls into the categories of emergent care; detoxification, prenatal care, perinatal care, or psychiatric care, get to the assessment site as soon as possible as these classifications increase your loved one's chance of getting into a treatment center that day.

If after you have completed the assessment and someone tells you that your loved one is not eligible for treatment, you must become a strong advocate for your family. I once was trying to help an individual get into treatment who was not in a priority population, had been in seven treatment centers previously (three inpatient treatments that year), and would only go to one particular treatment facility. The SCA was not going to fund this individual's treatment.

The family then called their local county commissioner and the SCA immediately changed their mind and agreed to pay for this individual's drug and alcohol treatment. So, if you have your back against the wall and you are being told "No," call your commissioner, congressman, or senator. Make noise and you will improve your chances of getting into treatment.

I would like to take a moment here to interject something. Some treatment facilities will present you an option of paying for treatment out of pocket. This means they are not going to deny services to your loved one but you need to set up a payment plan that you will pay 100 percent on your own. Families will go for this option because they believe the life of the loved one is priceless. I have seen families take out additional mortgages on their homes, open lines of credit wherever they can, liquidate 401k's, savings accounts and stocks. Before exploring those options, my suggestion would be to look into changing your insurance plans or even insurance companies when appropriate.

I am not one to tell a person how they should spend their money but my experience suggests that there is another treatment center out there that will accept your loved one without your having to liquidate every asset that you have. I know the ideal treatment center would be local so the family can be more involved but talk with facilities about scholarship programs and see if they provide referrals to treatment centers in other states.

Going to the Intake/Assessment

O.K., you figured out the insurance and you are set to go to your intake/assessment appointment. Here is what to expect at an intake/assessment.

The appointment will be with a trained professional assessor. In an ideal world you will walk in at a scheduled time and be seen promptly by the assessor and the intake/assessment will be completed within 90 minutes. You will be briefed by the assessor at the end of the assessment for 15 minutes about recommendations and next steps. While being briefed, your insurance is being approved for the recommended level of care and you will either leave with a scheduled appointment to meet your counselor (for outpatient treatment) or depending on the recommendation, your loved one will be admitted right away into an inpatient facility.

Now that we understand the steps for the intake/assessment process and have narrowed down where we need to go for the assessment, the next question I usually hear from a concerned loved one is, "How do we walk with somebody through this process?"

The first thing that you will need to do once the intake appointment is scheduled is determine who will go with your loved one to the assessment site. The addict/alcoholic should be accompanied by somebody close to them such as a family member. This helps ensure arrival to the intake appointment and that your loved one's intake questions are accurately answered.

Also, if a document is forgotten at home, the family member can go home and get it. When waiting for the assessment to begin, there will be some initial paperwork that needs to be filled out before meeting somebody face to face for an assessment. You can also help assist your loved one in filling out these documents.

Next up will be the assessment. Your loved one will be going into the assessment by themselves as this will be the most effective and efficient evaluation process. You most certainly can request to sit in for some of the assessment, however, this tends to slow the process down. If you choose to sit in on the assessment, I believe it is best to agree to sit in at the end of the assessment and express your concerns and go over the conclusion and recommendations during this time.

You may choose to express your concerns at the beginning of the assessment but I would encourage you to be direct and to the point. This is a very emotional time and you have been through a lot to get to this point. Due to this added and sometimes unnoticed stress, a family member wants to give all the information they have; however, this slows down the assessment process and prevents your loved one from entering treatment as fast as possible.

My encouragement is that if you need to talk before the evaluation, keep concerns direct and limited to cover concerns such as a Mental Health diagnosis, a recent overdose or any other possible life threatening situations. When you, your loved one and the assessor meet at the end of the assessment, you will have the opportunity to discuss with them your concerns for your loved one as well as the outcome of the assessment. At this time, the assessor will also be able to tell you the best way that you can support your loved one.

Upon completion of an assessment, a recommendation will be given for a level of treatment for your loved one. For the sake of our discussion, let's say that they are recommended to enter an inpatient detox unit. Excellent! This is the level of treatment that you were hoping for and you are very happy! Note here, if you were hoping for this result, take a small bag of clothes to the assessment so your loved one can take this with them to the inpatient facility.

Important

The next step you can do to help your loved one is to make sure they safely arrive and are admitted to the inpatient facility. This may consist of you physically driving them to the treatment facility or it may take you waiting with them until the treatment facility can come and pick them up and drive them to their facility.

Please, if you are the one transporting them to the inpatient facility **do not stop for anything.**

Drive them directly to the facility. There is nothing that is more important that they need to do right now than to get to the treatment facility in the same condition they were in at the assessment. If they need an article of clothing, etc., you can drop whatever they need off at the facility later. I have worked with hundreds of individuals who will promise to enter an inpatient facility tomorrow or a week from now. I would refrain from waiting, as this is a time-sensitive matter. They could lose their spot at the facility, they may no longer meet criteria to enter the facility and there is a whole slew of other factors that could come into play. Please, just get them to the facility. You have taken this much time to get your loved one approved for a treatment facility, Don't break the momentum. Keep on keepin' on, and go right to the facility and into treatment.

Congratulations--your loved one is admitted by the inpatient facility! This may be the first time that you can actually think about yourself. This has been a long process and now maybe for the first time in a long time you can breathe!

Upon arriving at home you have one more important task to complete. Go through the house, rooms, cars, basement, etc., and clean out any alcohol and get rid of any drugs and paraphernalia. I hate to see good effort and good money go to waste when an addict is on their first night home from treatment and finds a bag or a bottle of booze. I have a friend who spent the full 30 days in an inpatient facility and, unfortunately, his wife was not willing to get rid of her wine collection. Within one week, my friend was drinking again.

Now more than ever, it is so important for you to take stock of your condition and determine how best to rejuvenate and revitalize yourself. Your loved one will be going through many changes while in inpatient treatment. As they're learning new skills, this is a time for you to learn what they are learning and this may be a time where you'll need to learn some new skills yourself. Having a support group is extremely important. Suggestions on support groups will be covered in more detail in the next chapter

Right now is your opportunity to regroup and revitalize yourself. Your loved one is in treatment and safe. This may be the first time in a long time that you feel that you know your loved one is safe and you just might be able to rest easily. Do something to celebrate. Be kind to yourself! This may be the time to take a vacation, get back to going to the gym, take a "me" day off work, or treat yourself to a nice dinner. It is always important to celebrate accomplishments in life and you are a BIG reason as to why your loved one is in a safe environment. You are giving them the opportunity to find a way out of their addiction and alter their life. It's time to celebrate how your love and commitment has paid off.

6
Taking Care Of Yourself

"In any given moment we have two options:
to step forward into growth or to
step back into safety."
--Abraham Maslow

I stated before that one of the most frequent questions I get asked is, "How do I walk with someone through treatment?" The absolute best way to support someone through treatment is by getting yourself in the best mental, physical and spiritual condition possible. Start by having a primary focus to love and rejuvenate yourself.

I invite you to participate in the following exercise to help you stay in good mental, physical and spiritual health. On this page or on a separate piece of paper write out your responses to these following steps:

1) Write down five people you can talk to about anything.

2) Next write three things you can do every week to help your body stay healthy, i.e., eat an apple every day.

3) Now write down three things you can do each week to help develop and nourish your spiritual life, i.e., read pages out of a spiritual book three times a week.

4) Lastly, and this is crucial, write out a commitment that you will tell two of the people in Step one everything you wrote in Steps two and three.

When confiding in your chosen two people, open the door to allow them to check in with you every 30 days about your progress. If you follow through on this exercise you will be amazed at how much better your life will get and how much better you will feel.

Now that you have completed this exercise I want to take a moment and talk about support groups. Your loved one is currently being encouraged to engage in a support group and I am encouraging you to engage in a support group. The most effective support groups are the 12-step based groups such as Al-Anon or Nar-Anon. These are family groups for loved ones who have been impacted by somebody struggling with an addiction. Now, no one will go through exactly what you are going through because every situation is unique; however, benefits of these groups include meeting other people who have similar stories to yours and can relate to and identify feelings and emotions that you have experienced. You will also learn about the 12 steps, which is a process that your loved one is currently being educated on while in treatment. Al-Anon recommends that you attend a minimum of six meetings before deciding whether to stop attending these meetings or to continue.

A note of encouragement here is that many times when we are doing something that makes us feel uncomfortable it may be the very thing that we need to do in order to be successful. If after attending six meetings you feel that these groups are not for you, please find a support group that you will attend. There are great support groups through your churches, temples or community centers. The key is that you are engaging in a group and that you do not have to do all of this alone. Worth Repeating: You do not have to do it all alone. You may find your support group in karate, yoga or a book club. It is imperative to incorporate a community support group in your life, as your loved one's recovery process is a lifelong adventure. There will be highs and lows and as long as you're in fit mental, physical, emotional, spiritual and behavioral condition you will be able to be the best help for your loved one, as well as for yourself through this recovery process.

Many of us have been so entrenched in helping our loved one enter treatment that we do not even realize how time consuming this has become. Our loved one has occupied so much of our thoughts and time that we become almost nervous when there is quiet, peace or down time and we are unsure what to do. When we are engaged in a support group, others help us walk that line between being consumed with our loved one and taking care of our self.

In Appendix A, you will find the 12 steps of Alcoholics Anonymous listed. This is just the introduction to the beginning of your understanding of what the 12 steps mean. I will go more in depth into the 12 step program and fellowship in Chapter 9. For now, I feel that this is a good place to start and that you can utilize this page as a talking point when you introduce yourself to others at an Al-Anon meeting. You will find that as you ask questions of other attendees at the meetings, they will be more than happy to answer them and help in any way they can.

Some of you reading this book may have already engaged in the 12-step process before. Some of the support people you have met in these programs could come with you to the intake/assessment or even check in with a phone call to you while you are waiting for your loved one's assessment or entrance to the treatment facility.

This leads us into the next section which talks about small steps you can take that will have a huge impact in walking alongside your loved one while they are in treatment. Since we already know the levels of treatment (as covered in Chapter 4) I will begin by discussing a few keys to help with engagement in an inpatient facility and quickly move to discussing how you can stand beside and help someone who is in a general outpatient program. How you can walk alongside someone in general outpatient will relate to how you can do this with every level of care.

Just as we have spent this last chapter looking at a plan to develop your self-care, when your loved one steps down from each level of treatment they will have a list of goals and strategies on how they can continue a self-care plan. Generally, these are referred to as discharge plans or aftercare plans. These plans will become great resources for you and your loved one as you continue to forge this team approach to their recovery.

7
Walking With Someone In Treatment

"If you always put limits on everything you do, physical or anything else. It will spread into your work and into your life. There are no limits. There are only plateaus, and you must not stay there, you must go beyond them."
--Bruce Lee

Every family system is unique. You and your loved one are the experts on how your daily living routines work. You are the ones who are going to be able to determine proper goals and action steps that are realistic to you and your family situation. The more groundwork that is accomplished while in inpatient treatment the easier the transition will be for your loved one when they leave the inpatient facility.

You may wonder what is happening while your loved one is in an inpatient facility. Many facilities have something called black-out time. This means your loved one has no contact with the outside world for three days or even seven days. Even though they cannot contact you, you are encouraged to contact the treatment center to see how your loved one is doing. So how can you actively support them during their treatment? I would like to discuss practical ways to accomplish this goal.

While in inpatient treatment, your loved one is going to have weekly individual sessions. Since you know they will be having an individual session, reach out to the treatment center and ask to schedule a family session. This way you can openly discuss struggles and successes your loved one is having. Many parents or spouses with whom I assist get confused because they do not understand why a counselor does not just tell them *everything* that is being discussed with their loved one. Due to best practices and confidentiality laws, a counselor is not able to do this. It is our loved one's right not to have the counselor disclose to you anything that is going on in treatment but when you have a family session you can inquire about goals and progress. This will open the door for your loved one and the counselor to tell you what is really going on in treatment and what progress is being made.

Many people think that if they are unable to physically attend, a family session is impossible. This is a common misconception. You can always set up a conference call during the scheduled session time and this way everybody can get on the same page. The more involved you are in your loved one's treatment, the more you are going to be able to help and support them. You're going to know what their goals are, how they plan to achieve them and how you can best support them upon their discharge from treatment. Being on the same page as your loved one and the counselor helps your loved one be successful and significantly reduces the chances of any surprises or miscommunication.

Now is a perfect time for everyone to lean on the counselor for boundary setting. For instance, ask the counselor to provide examples of successful accountability boundaries set by other families. Upon completion of inpatient treatment there are going to be natural expectations and goals that your loved one will need to fulfill. Proactive, proper boundary setting in inpatient treatment will take away any excuses upon returning home for not accomplishing these obligations.

This theme of working together in treatment, your new partnership, should continue as your loved one steps down from inpatient to PHP to IOP to general outpatient (GOP). Before we continue with discussing how you can walk alongside your loved one in treatment I want to reinforce the importance of a support group for you and your loved one. Your loved one will be encouraged to join a support group after they are discharged from the inpatient facility and since you are not currently in an inpatient facility you should seek to join a support group as well. I encourage you to make attending support groups a part of your loved ones treatment plan. Since you are leading by example, it will make it easier for your loved one to attend groups as well.

Now, switching gears, let us say that your loved one steps immediately down to GOP instead of PHP or IOP. Your loved one will need to attend one individual session a week that lasts one hour. Now the question is what else will your loved one engage in in conjunction with the GOP? For example, is the individual also going to attend a group session at the treatment center? Typically, group sessions are an hour-and-a-half long. Are they going to attend a 12-step meeting? This may include Al-Anon, Alcoholics Anonymous (AA), Narcotics Anonymous (NA), Overeaters Anonymous (OA) and Sexaholics Anonymous (SA). As you can see, there are multiple anonymous groups one can attend and we will go more in depth into 12-step programs in Chapter 9.

School-aged addict/alcoholic

Another option could be to involve a school counselor if this is age-appropriate but this tends to be a struggle because of the stigma behind seeing a school counselor. The thought of the embarrassment that an adolescent may experience when the rest of their classmates find out, can be unbearable. Also, the reality is most guidance counselors are not equipped to address addictions. Many school systems contract out drug and alcohol counseling services. You may be better off contacting those service centers directly.

It is important to realize that to attend treatment just one hour a week for an individual/family session rarely is enough to effectively address the problem. Many people fall into the trap of thinking that their loved one is in treatment and that this one hour a week session is going to cure them. This is a false sense of complacency. There are other changes that need to occur.

In the beginning stage of any level of treatment, an often-overlooked tool is goal-setting. I have mentioned before the necessity for goal-setting in inpatient treatment. Goal-setting is a priority in all levels of treatment and change can be achieved most rapidly in a successful outpatient treatment program.

Setting realistic, attainable goals is key to successful achievement. Within the first three individual sessions, your loved one should have worked in collaboration with their counselor to outline treatment goals they want to accomplish in the next 30, 60, 90, days. Hopefully they are also setting goals for the next six months and the next year as well. Those who are future- focused, will look at goals for five years and 10 years, but this may be overwhelming for some people as it can be difficult enough just to stay sober one day at a time.

It is important that your loved one is setting goals with their counselor. If your loved one is left to setting their own goals, this could lead to their trying to do too much too fast and ultimately failing. I have known several clients who have left treatment facilities with instructions and agreed-upon goals to follow the direction of just five key activities every day (i.e., going to a meeting, calling a member of their support network, etc.); however, these clients ended up adding and adding to their list and were soon attempting to do 20+ activities a day. It became too overwhelming for them and they just stopped doing everything and went back to using.

As part of your loved one's support network, you can meet for a family session and discuss goals. This will allow you to go over the goals that have been agreed upon and to quickly discover any discrepancies that you may have between what you and your loved one's agreed-upon goals are and the goals the loved one is setting forth in treatment. When you are involved in goal-setting then you know how to support the goals of the individual. In short, it allows everybody to come together in agreement and move forward as a team. When everyone is on the same page you can have realistic expectations, develop a tailored program to help support your loved one and know how to set proper boundaries while keeping each other accountable.

Warning sign: If a counselor does not want to have a family session, there is a problem. Find out immediately why they do not want to have a family session. This is worth a direct call to the facility. Then, I would suggest immediately having a family session or switching counselors. There are in some extreme cases reasons not to have a family session and one of those cases would be in the case of abuse. In these extreme cases, I strongly suggest you seek treatment for yourself and make sure that you are receiving some communication on how you can best support your loved one.

Each party involved may have to adjust their schedule to create a time for a family session but everyone should be willing to make some sort of compromise, as it is the life of the addict/alcoholic and the family unit that is on the line. Everyone involved only wants the best for your loved one.

In outpatient treatment, my encouragement is to have a minimum of one family session a month. This allows everybody to discuss and measure progress for 30, 60, 90 days. This may seem like a long period of time right now. I assure you the time will pass by quickly. The benefits of doing this are that everyone stays on the same page, gets to discuss the successes of goals that have been achieved, add new goals and become aware of the overall progress.

During these family sessions, you will have a better idea of whether your loved one is able to arrest their addiction and change behavior. Behavior can be changed (or even masked) for a month or two. However, it's long-lasting change that we are looking for. So, please, <u>even after 90 days my encouragement is to stay in treatment</u>. **We know (from millions of hours of experience) that the longer someone**

51

stays in treatment the more likely they are to have long-term sobriety.

Counseling sessions are only a part of treatment when addressing the individual and the changes they are looking to make. The more we can rally a community around the addict/alcoholic, the more successful they will be. In addition to the counseling, a priest, a minister, a rabbi, a religious leader, a mentor, or a karate instructor may be the additional support the individual needs. Letting your loved one choose another influential and positive role model who they will see in addition to the counselor is <u>important</u>. They will be more likely to take ownership over this commitment and relationship and hopefully the person will be somebody you can agree upon. Again, if they are meeting with somebody other than their counselor, it would be helpful to have in writing what they are working on and some of their goals or life rules. Written communication takes out the ambiguity and the all too often miscommunication and false expectations one can have. These false expectations often result in heated arguments and misunderstandings, ultimately leading to resentments and excuses to go back to using.

You know your loved one very well. You'll be the first one to know that things are changing for the positive. It has a lot to do with observations. You have become a master at observation, as this is the skill which brought you to the point that you knew deep down inside that your loved one needed to change.

During this time in outpatient treatment there are also things that you could be doing to help keep your loved one accountable. I make the strong suggestion for random drug testing. Again, if someone is not using, then there's no problem for him or her to take a drug test. Suspicion will come if they refuse to have a drug test. I worked with an individual for a nine-month period and after the first three months we stopped administering urine drug screens (UDS). The family, the client and I agreed to stop the drug screens as they were costly and the family was trying to save money. At nine months, we were ready to discharge and the client took a UDS. At this point the client came clean and advised that he had been using for the past six months.

Drug tests are one of the many tools that help us gauge the person's progress. They are not the "end all, be all" but in this instance if I had been giving random drug screens then we *may* have been able to address the active using sooner. Again, worth repeating, drug testing is just a tool, a generally reliable objective tool in a situation rife with deceit, impulsivity and overall good intention. It also immediately diffuses those circular conversations that start with "You don't believe me..."

Another action you can take during this time is a spot check of rooms, computers, cars, and any places where the addict/alcoholic may be hiding something. They might not appreciate the intrusion; however, they need to come to their own realization that their past actions brought them to this point. Something they did also brought us to this point of having to check and you are not a fan of having to do this but you are willing to go through this to help your loved one through whatever they need to go through. If you can do this, it becomes a "no brainer" for accountability and eliminates the temptations for the addict to "hold onto" something for a "rainy day."

Now, more than ever, don't stop setting and keeping boundaries. Yes, they are difficult to keep. Yes, your loved one may be sober for a month or two but it probably took a long time for you to get them into treatment. Your loved one needs to understand that it's going to take some time to build up certain levels of trust. It's a simple formula. It took a long time to break the trust, now it takes a long time to build that trust back up. Part of trust building needs to be the addict's willingness to trust you by letting you look in their car, rooms, etc. You may hear the arguments: "How can I ever change if you don't believe me?" or "Nobody trusts me anyway so I may as well do something to be accused of." Remember you are not accusing them of anything. You are just helping them stay accountable and keeping a healthy boundary. Remind them that it has taken, in some cases, many years, for the addiction to rear its head. Maybe it will take that many years to build back up that trust.

This may be a conversation that is best had with the help of a third party such as a counselor. It is not them you mistrust, it is the disease, and you don't need to apologize to anyone for that.

I really want to take a moment here to take my hat off to you and congratulate you (you should take a moment and congratulate yourself!) on getting this far. I know it has been difficult and there has been a lot of sacrifice on your part. There may have been intense fighting back-and-forth but you continued to push on! Congratulate yourself! Your love and perseverance are working. Maybe at this point we can begin to see that our greatest challenges force us to grow the most. Your loved one will draw support from the same love and determination that you have been demonstrating. You are an example for them about what showing up in life, and walking in love and kindness is all about. It is better known as practicing what you preach. Please remember that you are not responsible for their choices, just as no one is responsible for your choices. These positive actions you are taking will hopefully continue to influence your loved one to make the right choices.

One of the best teachers in life is observing the manner in which other individuals walk through life. My second child walked faster than my first, as they had someone to watch how it was done. When people show us what to do, we learn faster. Through your loved one's observations of you, you are giving them the permission and the freedom to go ahead and let their love shine. Thank you for being you and please treat yourself to an ice cream cone or a nice fancy dinner.

This chapter has effective suggestions that I have seen work in my years in the addiction field. There are many more great examples of things that you can do and if you have any suggestions I encourage you to write to me and let me know what worked for you. I also encourage you to share these successes with other families who are walking through this addiction epidemic as we can be the best supports and resources for one another.

I will end this chapter with this. Studies show that these three things are correlated to an individual's effective long-term recovery; 1) family involvement in treatment, 2) attending a meeting immediately upon discharge from an inpatient facility (or at least that day), and 3) remaining in treatment for a minimum of six months.

8
What To Do After Treatment

"Forgiveness is not just about the other. It's
for the beauty of your soul. It's for your
own capacity to fulfill your life."
--Jack Kornfield

Upon completing a treatment program,
celebrate! A change has occurred and the
commitment of staying in treatment in a sober state
has been fulfilled. Excellent. It is a miracle for any
addict to stay sober 24 hours let alone this length of
time. Take time to acknowledge the moment and
accomplishment. Enjoy it! Celebrate the fact that
achievement resulted from taking action, following a
plan and accomplishing goals!

While enjoying the accomplishment, make sure
you have goals and a game plan for moving forward
intact. Everyone needs to keep a copy of the discharge
plans completed before leaving treatment handy,
since this will have customized goals outlined. Now
that treatment is over and your loved one is feeling
better, don't stop-- keep on keepin' on--the recovery
is just beginning.

All too often what I see happen at this point in a person's recovery is that they will stop doing the very things that produced success and helped them to get this far in their recovery process. I believe it is human nature to rest on our laurels, to stop doing the very things that created success for us.

Aware of this potential downfall, you now have the opportunity to help your loved one continue to be successful, fulfilling their goals and leading a productive, happy life. You know the way out.

Following treatment, sticking to a schedule is ESSENTIAL. Routine, structure and discipline are HUGE for somebody in addiction. The good thing is that you've been working on a routine and a schedule ever since your loved one entered treatment. This is their schedule and they should be invested in it. Not feeling "in the zone" every day is quite common. It is good to remind all concerned that feelings are not facts and that feeling like using doesn't mean you have to use. Make no mistake though. This period after treatment is a critical phase of someone's recovery.

Part of their schedule needs to be engagement in a support group. I do suggest engaging in a 12-step program. First, they are free. Second, there are many meetings in your area (wherever your area) and are almost too convenient to choose not to attend. Third, they provide an instant support group for your loved one. Your loved one may not like all the people at the meetings or what's talked about, and that's a good (normal) thing. Remember when you were in high school? You did not like everybody in high school, so there will undoubtedly be different personalities that your loved one will have to adjust to. This is great practice for learning how to get along with others at work or in the community and a great practice in learning what patience and tolerance of other people really means.

Remember the phrase, "Recovery is a lifelong process." Just because the formal treatment program is complete does not mean everyone is "all better." Your loved one may not have ingested a substance in their body for a period of time but there are some personality characteristics that need to be worked out. Otherwise, they tend to return to their addictive substance. More than "tend to": It is almost a guarantee.

A key principle is that the substance was the *solution* to life's problems. There is a need to build other solutions into their lives so they can address the problems life will throw at them. This is not meant to scare you. Recovery literature says a person has recovered from a hopeless state of mind and body and that is true!; however, it is more accurate to say addiction to something has been put into remission. If a clean and sober individual were to pick back up again, they would quickly return to a hopeless state of mind, body and spirit. Our goal is not only to help the addict to stop ingesting substances but to be happy and free in their mind as well. Remember this is a disease that affects the mind, body and spirit.

A powerful suggestion I have for you is to start writing a gratitude list every day. For three-and-a-half years, I wrote a gratitude list every morning of 10 things for which I was grateful. While sitting down with my cup of coffee, I would take two minutes and write out: I am grateful for …, I am grateful for…. The things I was grateful for at any moment could range from the color blue, to music, to my relationship with God. During this period of my life people consistently asked me why I was so happy. Not knowing what to tell people, I would say thank you and engage in conversations about my daily routines and their daily routines. I realized that I had a different view of life and I was not really sure why but I believe it had to do with a combination of factors that included routines like this..

So, at three-and-a-half years what did I do? I stopped writing my gratitude list that took me no more than two minutes every morning. I could not see it at the time but my attitude gradually started to change from a positive attitude to an "Uhh, that's life" mentality. From this attitude, I would find myself seeing the negative in most situations first! I am happy to say that when I started writing this book I began writing a gratitude list again, mostly every day. I know it works and I know it changes the way I see the world.

However, there are days that I still say "I don't want to do it. It takes too much time to write that down." I am slowly working on getting myself better. Slow and steady wins the race, and people who make gratitude lists do better than those who don't.

We can build on the momentum you have created reading the book thus far. Embrace this moment and write in the space below 10 things you are grateful for. You can do this and I know you can! I will help you start writing your first two sentences:

I am grateful for ...

I am grateful for....

9
What Is This 12-Step Program?

"Rarely have we seen a person fail who has
thoroughly followed our path."
--Alcoholics Anonymous

Today's clinically accepted recovery practices, now emphasize addressing the social circles you are immersed in as well as the mind, body and spirit. Alcoholics Anonymous encompasses and addresses all of these concerns.

Naturally you are asking yourself, "What is this 12-step program that I see on TV or hear about in the treatment centers?" Bill Wilson and Dr. Bob Smith are the originators of the AA 12-step program and what we call today Alcoholics Anonymous. Alcoholics Anonymous is a free program and fellowship founded in 1935, and it was not until 1939 that the book "Alcoholics Anonymous" was published. This basic text includes the outline for the 12 steps of Alcoholics Anonymous (see Appendix A). Many 12-step members will summarize the program as "practicing these principles in all our affairs." By practicing these principles, the hope is to break the strongholds that were influenced by the addiction.

These 12-step principles require that you utilize self-will to take an introspective look at yourself. These principles are a reminder that putting down the substances is but a start. A big start, but just a start.

Naturally, none of us are too excited about taking an in-depth look at ourselves. Identifying and taking ownership of our strengths and weaknesses is challenging work. I believe this challenge is magnified in somebody who is new in recovery. Most addicts are beyond comprehending living a life *not* filled with shame and guilt. The overwhelming majority of the individuals I have worked with acknowledge that by the time they admit the addiction is a problem for them, they have already resigned themselves to the fact that life cannot be different and that this way of life, *that they do not enjoy*, is where they are called to be--with no way out. This is an unimaginable and horrible way to live. For someone in addiction this is a common, hopeless outlook on life.

The 12-step recovery program and fellowship will remove this hopeless feeling and provide direction to a way out. The program works. People who have addictions outside of alcohol have also sought to adopt this model because they know it works. There are more than 258 fellowships and support groups that have been formed based upon the AA fellowship and program. Imitation is the sincerest form of flattery.

The 12 steps are not for somebody to try to understand before they actually follow them. AA is a program of action. This is a common stumbling block for people and it is often the cause as to why addicts will not start or follow through on the steps. "Rarely have we seen a person fail who has thoroughly followed our path." By trying to intellectually figure out the steps, many people come to the conclusion that "12-step programs do not work." Sadly, this leads addicts to leave the program, search for another program, or continue to try and figure this thing out on their own. (One can get the benefit of doing the steps without understanding how and why they work.)

Trying to figure out how the steps work before doing them would be like trying to figure out the flight process before getting on an airplane. I was a flight attendant and if I had to figure that out I would never had gone aboard! No one would ever get on the airplane if that were the case. We just have to get on board and trust in the process as we go through everything from check in, to boarding, to take off, in flight, landing, exiting the plane, and picking up our luggage. This would be very exhausting if I had to figure out how all this works and then try to make sense of it and not disagree with how my luggage gets to Honolulu, Hawaii, when I have a connecting flight in Timbuktu.

Conversely, I wouldn't want an untrained pilot to get in the cock pit and say, "I'll figure this out as I go." We need information and good advice, but it only bears fruit when we put it into practice.

Luckily there were people who went before us on these airplanes and now we have so much confidence in flying that we do not second-guess it. We now get the benefit of air travel without understanding how to fly a plane.

With the steps, you must go through the process in order to really understand it. That's how we have a solid, successful experience.

The other objection most people have for not wanting to be a part of a 12-step recovery group is because of the God/Higher Power concept of the program. In a world driven by the concept of spirituality, it seems this is almost a silly argument as to why someone would not get involved in a 12-step program. The overwhelming majority of humanity agrees that something is in charge of the universe. Who, when in bitter despair, has not called out to something beyond themselves for help? For this chapter and for the purposes of the AA/NA program let's just call this something "God or Higher Power."

The 12-step program emphasizes the need to develop a relationship with God/Higher Power. You may have been raised in a traditional religion or belief. Build upon what you know or start exploring a new loving belief. The key is to have a RELATIONSHIP with a power greater than yourself. This concept is scary to many individuals since this puts an emphasis on the need to make your own personal decision as to what your Higher Power is. This is a place of great discovery for your loved one. One that is easily balked at because there is effort that is needed to develop a relationship with a higher power.

The addict may say, "I am an atheist and can not be a part of this 12-step group. Did you know that there are Atheist Churches! I know I was amazed when I heard this, too. It makes me think that even if I were an atheist I see the power in being in community.

There is certainly a bit of irony in that someone whose life is spinning out of control to the extent that they need medication or hospitalization, have trouble at work (if they work) or might not even shower regularly, won't accept help because of the "God" word.

For the addict who is an atheist or agnostic, GOD can mean Good Orderly Direction. Encourage your loved one to take the good orderly direction and utilize their Higher Power as taking direction from the 12 steps. Do not let God be the cop-out for not wanting to put forth the effort to work the program. Step 12 reads "Having had a spiritual awakening as **the** result of these steps, we tried to carry this message to addicts and to practice these principles in all our affairs." This very last step says that you will have a spiritual experience if you go through the steps. So let the Higher Power in your program be the steps if you need to. Again, it is a process that you need to walk through and experience yourself.

If your loved one is adamant that they will not go to a 12-step program, please make sure they are staying connected and accountable in an introspective program that includes a sociocultural component, as well as addressing the health of the mind, body and spirit. AA takes the stance that they are not the only way to get sober; however, it has worked for millions of people. If your loved one is in a 12-step program but is refusing to do the steps, then I urge you to set a boundary with them. If a person went to an inpatient facility and continued to use, we wouldn't be O.K. with that. Then we ought not to be O.K. with our loved one bypassing the steps while going to a 12-step program.

In regard to building a support network and learning about these principles, an individual is not supposed to do this alone. The suggestion is to have a sponsor. AA has written a pamphlet on sponsorship and I encourage you to pick up a copy or read it for free online. Here are a few suggestions I have regarding asking someone to be your sponsor. A sponsor should be someone who has at least one year of continuous sobriety, has been through the 12 steps, continues to work the steps in their daily lives, and males should work with males and females work with females.

Again, there are no rules in 12 step but there are some musts and suggestions. I believe a sponsor can be a mentor; however, the main objective of a sponsor is to take their sponsee (the addict) through the steps. May they form a friendship? Sure! May further advice happen? Sure... but it may not. That is why the addict also needs to make friends in the fellowship. Relying on the sponsor as the one and only contact point is not a good idea. People make mistakes. If your loved one can get a sponsor and make many sober friends in 12 step, then they will have a better chance of staying sober. Think about animal packs. The babies are in the middle of the pack and stay surrounded by the mature adults so that less harm will come to them. Have your loved one stay in the middle of the pack and they will do well.

I have only skimmed the surface on what 12-step programs of love and service have to offer. I have a friend who "worked the steps" as he related it to sugar! He did what any member of a 12-step group should do, he started on the introspective adventure of going through the 12 steps and had a spiritual experience.

If you are inclined to read more about the 12-step program, I suggest you read the article, "The Next Frontier: Emotional Sobriety," by Bill Wilson, co-founder of AA. I have also included the 12 Traditions of Alcoholics Anonymous in Appendix B. Lastly, I strongly suggest reading an experienced medical doctor's opinion about alcoholism and Alcoholics Anonymous by reading the Doctor's Opinion in the preface of the book Alcoholics Anonymous.

Please use the next page to write down any contact numbers you may get of people in 12 step or even utilize the page to keep notes on the Al-Anon and/or Nar-Anon meetings that you will attend.

"We commenced to search out the things in ourselves which had brought us to physical, moral, and spiritual bankruptcy."
--Bill Wilson

10
Repairing Relationships

"Life has taught us that love does not consist
of gazing at each other, but in looking
outward together in the same direction."
--Antoine de Saint-Exupery

Beyond addressing the addiction, recovery includes re-establishing and repairing relationships. This disease not only damages material possessions, it also causes emotional scarring in relationships. Repairing relationships, like the individual's recovery, can be a lifelong process. At the core of repairing relationships is building trust.

I realize the most terrifying question you may be asking yourself is, "How can a relationship be repaired if my loved one starts using again?" It is true; some return to active addiction, but others do not. So, why not take a chance on the immense joy you can have in this rebuilt relationship?

Since all relationships are grounded in trust, I suggest starting there. Start small and build. "Go slow, go far." Relationships have rules. Whether you are married or have a best friend, there are some underlying rules in your relationship. For example, if you are married you would have committed to wedding vows. When setting goals during treatment, rules were established and maybe a contract between you and your loved one was signed while your loved one was in treatment. If there is no contract, try making a small agreement. For example, "I trust you to take out the garbage every Tuesday." Over time, you can evaluate if this habit becomes second nature or if it is something for which your loved one needs encouragement.

The two of you may disagree on this process. Your loved one may ask, "How can I move forward if nobody trusts me?" Having them in your home or in many cases being back in your life, is evidence of your trust. It may be necessary to point out that it has taken X number of years for them to seek treatment, so it may take just as long to regain all that trust. Go slow, go far. THIS IS NOT A SPRINT, IT'S A LONG DISTANCE RACE. Do not run in vain. In this race, you will need to help each other in order to stay on the right path and to keep moving in the right direction. Run in such a way that you win.

This trust process can be likened to the relationship between Ronald Reagan and Mikhail Gorbachev during the Cold War. Gorbachev said "You do not trust me." Reagan said, "Of course I do. Trust, but Verify." To do other than that is irresponsible.

Repairing relationships takes many forms: mental, emotional, physical, spiritual and behavioral.

These are the major components of a relationship and one doesn't come before another as they are all intertwined.

As with any relationship, communication is key. In fact, I suggest over-communicating. It may help if you list several goals/rules you have for yourself and the relationship with your loved one. For example, "There is an agreed-upon 10 P.M. curfew. If this curfew is broken, then you have chosen not to live in this house." Then you have to make sure you enforce that rule. Ask your loved one to set goals for themselves and for their relationship with you as well. This exercise helps the two of you to stay on the same page.

In addition to understanding one another's expectations, you will see whether your goals can be measured and whether the goals are realistic or even mutual. This allows for the creation of a deeper bond between the two of you as you have now given each other permission to encourage one another in achieving goals. Enjoy catching and letting your loved one know they are fulfilling their goals!

The great thing about repairing relationships is the joy and fun that you can experience once again. Often the joy is so intense because we sink to great depths during addiction and when we rise out of it, we are overwhelmed with jubilation. The appreciation for everyday life is fierce and the gratitude for the renewed relationship will be experienced at a higher level as well.

When your loved one returns home from treatment, they may want all of their relationships repaired immediately. Unfortunately, this is a dangerous and common expectation. The need for immediate gratification is a dominant trait of the addict/alcoholic. This entitlement thought process also highlights the need to change not just using habits but other habits and traits developed over time.

This may also be thought of as "all or nothing thinking." Helping your loved one realize that it takes time will be very beneficial. Again, it took a long time for your trust to be broken and it may take longer for that trust to be repaired. However, when your loved one knows you're on their side, and they're not alone, it helps tremendously and will build a stronger bond between you.

Part of repairing personal relationships includes repairing or building community relationships. Once treatment is finished, people often have a lot of time on their hands. An excellent way to fill this time is volunteering. Great places to start are hospitals, fire stations, police stations and local libraries. Although this may not be a first choice of how to spend one's time and there may be financial issues to address, your loved one can volunteer while they are applying for jobs. Not only is volunteering an excellent way to give back, but it also boosts self-esteem. Another bonus is that volunteering enhances a resume and at the same time will help to build trust as your loved one demonstrates a commitment to changing old behaviors.

11
Staying Connected

"Everything that irritates us about others can lead us to an understanding of ourselves."
--Carl Jung

I hope that you have found this book useful. I encourage you to make taking care of yourself Priority Number One. The oft cited example is correct, when you get on an airplane and the oxygen masks drop, you are instructed to put yours on first so you may be of help to others. You have digested some hard-to-swallow facts about yourself and your loved one, the complicated process of addiction and entering treatment. Breathe! It is the one thing we cannot live long without! Consciously taking a breath can slow things down, allowing us to respond rather than react, thereby giving us the ability to make clear, rational decisions.

I hope this book can serve as a guide that you can consult from time to time to remind you of the progress you have made. As difficult as it might be to believe, the struggles that led you to pick up this book can become important experiences in your life. When you continue to take care of your physical, emotional, and spiritual well-being, you will be able to love and help your loved one. In addition, you will be able to be open and vulnerable with others in pain because of their loved one's addiction. They can draw hope from your experience because they will see you've made it through and are living a fulfilling life.

Let's review some things discussed earlier:

We are responsible for our own happiness. We have been entangled and enmeshed with the addict and they have become part of our identity. Often, not knowing what we would do without the heightened chaos, we allowed this to become the norm in our lives. Through treatment, we have learned to set healthy boundaries/rules and no longer have to live by the whims and craziness of our addicted loved one.

Addiction is a disease. It cannot be cured but it can be arrested or put into remission. Although it may be scary, we must remember that once an addict puts a substance into their body, they have an adverse reaction and it overrides their basic instincts. It overrides the desire to eat, reproduce...survive. An addict may have weeks, months or years of sobriety but if they pick up again, it is only a matter of time (in most, cases, a very short period of time) before they are in full-blown addiction. This is not to suggest you live in fear that your loved one will return to using.

No! However, for everyone's happiness and safety, it is important to remember, they are not cured.

If you see a return to old habits, it is your responsibility to the relationship to mention it. For example, "I feel worried when I hear you are going to bars to watch football games." We are responsible for our own happiness, yet, at the same time, if we choose to remain in the addict's life, we need to keep the lines of communication and accountability open.

Many addicts have confided in me that they surrounded themselves with people they could manipulate in order to keep their addictions alive. If you begin to feel uncomfortable around the addict, confront them in a loving way. No one likes to be brow-beaten or accused, so remember to confront them in love. In fact, confronting them is the most loving thing you can do. As discussed earlier, keep the conversation in the "I" form, "I feel nervous when you stay up until 3 A.M and sleep until 1 P.M."

Relapse. Some say this is part of the recovery process. I know plenty of people who got sober the first time they tried and never picked up again. I admit they are the minority. That said, don't let the idea that relapse is part of the process be an excuse for your loved one to pick up. If you give permission for relapse, it will happen. If it does happen, don't give up. It doesn't have to be the ultimate defeat. Get up and get back to doing what was working for you to stay sober. Then, try to figure out the events and

77

thoughts that led to the relapse. Be unique and stay sober the first time.

I am all about beating the odds. Go for it. I am behind you. An inspiring thought is that if you have picked up this book then there is a high probability that your loved one has already attempted to get sober, so this time may be THE time they get sober.

Individuals show signs of relapse long before they pick up again. You know your loved one, so if you notice they are hanging out with the old crowd, lying, even about small things, falling back into old routines and not spending time with those who helped them get sober, recognize these as signs that someone may be headed toward relapse.

Your loved one has allowed you in their life in a vulnerable way for a reason. You have been a supporter of their recovery and have helped them stay accountable by following agreed-upon rules. Your loved one may not recognize these warning signs of relapse, so you owe it to yourself and them to be honest and point out what you see. After expressing your concerns to your loved one, discuss them with both your support networks.

The addict spends so much of their life hiding; there is no good reason to hide anymore. There is no reason to have to hide struggles, concerns and thoughts from one's support network. It takes a village to raise a person. Being honest is not "snitching." It may, in fact, save their life.

I know the difficulty in reaching out to others, so please start with me. My google contact number is 484-798-0336. Always leave a voice mail. I know that after you make that first outreach, the next outreaches will be a lot easier. I look forward to hearing from you and rejoicing in your successes or assisting you in any way I can.

12
Continuing With Success

"Peace I leave with you; my peace I give
you. I do not give to you as the world gives.
Do not let your hearts be troubled and do not
be afraid."
--John 14:27

One of the greatest measures of success is,
"How is your relationship today?" Most of those who
are reading this book will still have the addicted
person as part of their life. Please, remember there
are times when it's necessary to cut a person off in
your life especially when you feel emotional or
physical abuse is possible or has occurred. Remember
in those cases I strongly encourage you to seek safety
as well as professional help from the correct agencies.
It may be necessary for you to have a safety plan in
place and outlined for yourself to follow if you need to.
Remember, you can also dial 211 to find community
service agencies that can help you.

When you can look at the relationship with your
loved one objectively and say, "Yes, it is better than
it was a month ago, a year ago etc..." then you are on

the path to success. If you can answer truthfully to yourself that you are not preoccupied or consumed by what your addicted loved one is doing on a daily basis then you are probably on the right path. If you are unable to answer "yes" to those questions but you are able to feel at peace in this moment or even in the moment when you are with that person, then at least you know that YOU are getting better!

All of these processes that we have outlined are simple. Instinctively, they seem to make sense, however, I know they are not easy to implement. Much of the success of your loved one will be rooted in boundary-setting and holding to the boundaries we set. This is another reason why I will continue to urge you not to do this alone. Just as you do not want your loved one to walk through the addiction alone, neither should you have to walk through this change alone.

Families are a great resource. If you have the positive backing of the family, continue to utilize them. Many times we need the added support of our spiritual leaders, support groups, counselors and psychiatrists to give us the objective opinion we need.

As in everything worth doing there will be bumps in the road. More often than not when we begin taking action in a positive direction we feel those bumps in the road within weeks. I pray that those bumps do not discourage you too much. I know you can do it. Otherwise, you never would have made it to the end of this book.

You are now properly armed with the tools you

need to take care of yourself and to help someone else through this difficult journey in their life.

I hope you remember that if you feel you are not doing everything correctly, you are on the right path. You are moving in love because you love. When we make a few mistakes that is O.K. We sometimes just need to go back to doing the things that got us going in the right direction to begin with. Familiarity breeds complacency. No need to beat ourselves up and say, "We are not good enough" and "What is the use?" We have been doing that for far too long. Each day we need reminders of encouragement. Until this becomes second nature, I recommend you set a daily alarm on your phone that says, "Be kind to yourself; kindly, gently, patiently things are moving in a positive direction and you are beautiful." You can set as many alarms as you want. Come up with something that resonates with you and helps you stay in a healthy state of mind.

If there is a setback, this does not mean that we have to throw all the progress away that we made. Instead, let's build on the progress that we made and make it even better. Giving up is easy. Your journey so far has been difficult. When you work through the difficulty you give permission for others and yourself to shine. As others around you see that you are trudging through these difficulties, it might be the very thing that inspires them to continue to change in a positive direction. When we stick to the basics we are successful. Now we just need to get back to the basics of what works for each of us.

"To cling to the principles of the Judeo-Christian ethic--honesty, integrity compassion, love, ideas of hope, charity, humility --is an integral part of any person's life no matter what their position in life may be."
--Jimmy Carter

Epilogue

Thank you for your time in reading this book to completion and I trust that you have found this helpful. If you have additional comments or questions please reach out to me. I am open to scheduling sessions, family interventions as well as pointing you in the right direction if you are struggling with a loved one in need.

I hope this book serves as a guide for you in keeping yourself healthy while helping your family and your loved one through the treatment and recovery process.

Often when we start out on a new path, one of our first instincts is to second-guess ourselves and tell ourselves that we are doing it wrong and this is the wrong way to approach it. Please, trust in the process, as the process requires time. Give yourself those six Al- Anon meetings before you make a decision about continuing to attend and if you need to, let yourself have six more meetings before you make a final decision.

The recovery process is one that occurs over a lifetime and one that needs the help of a community. This community is essential to help with the biological, physiological and spiritual recovery of the addicted loved one. If you find yourself falling back into old habits, feeling complacent, or making mistakes. It's O.K., forgive yourself and get back to what worked to get you to this point. In my experience, the Number One reason why individuals diagnosed with bipolar disorder stop taking the medication that has helped stabilize them is because they felt better and did not think they needed to take the medication anymore. It's O.K., you are in good company. Many of us stop doing the very things that got us to the good points in our life. Remember, this does not mean you have lost all your progress. Pick back up from where you are and start doing the things you did to be successful and you are right back on that positive adventure path in life.

You hold the key to help someone enter treatment. Now it is up to them to follow your lead. If you have made it to the end of this book then I know you know of someone who needs help in entering treatment. You may be agonizing over the questions, "Am I enabling?" "Am I ignoring a problem?" "At what point will my loved one say, 'I am going to change?'" I believe by now you know if you are enabling or just ignoring a problem. Unfortunately, I cannot answer that last question for you. Each individual will come to their own point of wanting to change and for now all you can do is sow seeds into their life and believe they will see the benefit to change. As we plant these seeds in their lives our hope is they will grow up on fertile soil and blossom into becoming part of who they are. Inside the core of each of us, I know there is good. It has been calling out to us ever since we were young. Sometimes our life gets so overfilled that we have drowned out that voice of wanting to be better people. If we can get back to living by solid principles, enjoyment will flow. This light will flow through ourselves and in turn, others are touched with joy.

Let me help you help someone discover their inner joy again. Please, contact me with any questions or struggles you may have found in reading this book or in life. Remember, change happens in a moment and that moment is now.

Appendix A

The Twelve Steps of Alcoholics Anonymous

1) We admitted we were powerless over alcohol-- that our lives had become unmanageable.
2) Came to believe that a Power greater than ourselves could restore us to sanity.
3) Made a decision to turn our will and our lives over to the care of God *as we understood Him*.
4) Made a searching and fearless moral inventory of ourselves.
5) Admitted to God, to ourselves and to another human being the exact nature of our wrongs.
6) Were entirely ready to have God remove all these defects of character.
7) Humbly asked Him to remove our shortcomings.
8) Made a list of all persons we had harmed, and became willing to make amends to them all.
9) Made direct amends to such people wherever possible, except when to do so would injure them or others.
10) Continued to take personal inventory and when we were wrong promptly admitted it.

11) Sought through prayer and meditation to improve our conscious contact with God *as we understood Him*, praying only for knowledge of His will for us and the power to carry that out.

12) Having had a spiritual awakening as the result of these steps, we tried to carry this message to alcoholics and to practice these principles in all our affairs.

Appendix B

The Twelve Traditions of Alcoholics Anonymous

1) Our common welfare should come first; personal recovery depends upon AA unity.
2) For our group purpose there is but one ultimate authority--a loving God as He may express Himself in our group conscience. Our leaders are but trusted servants; they do not govern.
3) The only requirement for AA membership is a desire to stop drinking.
4) Each group should be autonomous except in matters affecting other groups or AA as a whole.
5) Each group has but one primary purpose--to carry its message to the alcoholic who still suffers.
6) An AA group ought never endorse, finance or lend the AA name to any related facility or outside enterprise, lest problems of money, property and prestige divert us from our primary purpose.
7) Every AA group ought to be fully self-supporting, declining outside contributions.
8) Alcoholics Anonymous should remain forever nonprofessional, but our service centers may employ special workers.

9)   AA, as such, ought never be organized; but we may create service boards or committees directly responsible to those they serve.

10)   Alcoholics Anonymous has no opinion on outside issues; hence the AA name ought never be drawn into public controversy.

11)   Our public relations policy is based on attraction rather than promotion; we need always maintain personal anonymity at the level of press, radio and films.

12)   Anonymity is the spiritual foundation of all our traditions, ever reminding us to place principles before personalities.

Appendix C

Withdrawal Symptoms Information Sheet

The bulk of these withdrawal symptoms will be present during the acute withdrawal phase and may include:	
• Tension • Panic attacks • Tremors • Difficulty concentrating • Short-term memory loss • Anxiety • Irritability • Diarrhea	• Disturbed sleep • Headache • Heart palpitations • Sweating • Nausea • Muscle pain and stiffness • Hypertension • Irregular heart rate

Other side effects of withdrawal include:	
• Depression • Insomnia • Nausea and vomiting • Irritability • Fatigue • Trouble concentrating • Muscle aches • Loss of appetite • Clammy skin	• Dizziness • Shakiness • Mood swings • Nightmares • Elevated heart rate • Tremors • Sweating • Loss of color in the face • Dehydration • Shallow breathing

Withdrawal symptoms mimic flu symptoms. The severity and duration of withdrawal is influenced by the level of dependency on the substance and a few other factors, including:

- Length of time abusing the substance

- Type of substance abused

- Method of abuse (e.g., snorting, smoking, injecting, or swallowing)

- Amount taken each time

- Family history and genetic makeup

- Medical and mental health factors

Withdrawal symptoms are generally over in one to two weeks. However Post Acute Withdrawal can last for weeks or even months.

Withdrawal Symptoms and Solutions

Symptoms	Cause	Duration	Relief
Constipation, stomach pain, gas	Intestinal movement decreases for a brief period.	1-2 weeks	• Drink plenty of fluids (more H2O the better) • Add fruits, vegetables, and whole-grain cereals to diet
Cough, dry throat, nasal drip	The body is getting rid of mucus, which has blocked airways and restricted breathing.	A few days	• Drink plenty of fluids • Avoid additional stress during the first few weeks
Depressed mood	It is normal to feel sad for a period of time after you first stop using. Many people have a strong urge to use when they feel depressed.	1-2 weeks	• Increase pleasurable activities • Talk with your clinician about changes in your mood • Get extra support from friends and family
Insomnia	*AOD affects brain wave	1 week	• Limit caffeine intake (and none after

	function and influences sleep patterns; coughing and dreams about using are common.		12 noon), because its effects will increase with stopping AOD use • Use relaxation techniques
Irritability	The body's craving for AOD can produce irritability.	2-4 weeks	• Take walks • Use relaxation techniques • Try hot baths
Craving for AOD	AOD are strongly addictive and withdrawal causes cravings	Frequent for 2-3 days ; can happen for months or years	• Wait out the urge, which lasts only a few minutes • Distract yourself • Exercise

* AOD stands for Alcohol and Other Drugs

Appendix D

Questions to Ask Insurer

Questions to ask your insurance company:

If services are In-Network:

- Do I have **behavioral health** benefits?
- Is **pre-certification** necessary?
- Is there a **deductible**?
- What is the **co-pay** (if any)?
- Is there a **limit** of sessions per year?
- Are the behavioral health **benefits** carved out to another entity?

If services are Out-of Network:

- Do I have **behavioral health** benefits?
- Is **pre-certification** necessary?
- What is the **deductible**?
- What **portion** does the insurance pay per session?
- Is there a **limit** of sessions per year?

References

Alcoholics Anonymous. 2001.4th ed. New York, NY:
Alcoholics Anonymous World Services, Inc.

American Psychological Association (2012). Stress in
American 2012 [Press release]. Retrieved
fromhttp://www.apa.org/news/press/releases
/stress/2012/generations.aspx

American Society of Addiction Medicine. 2011. Public
Policy Statement. Retrieved from
http://www.asam.org/docs/publicy-policy-
statements/1definition_of_addiction_long_4-
11.pdf?sfvrsn=2

American Society of Addiction Medicine. (2013). *The
ASAM criteria: Treatment criteria for
addictive, substance-related, and co-occuring
conditions.* Mee-Lee, D., Shulman, G.D.,
Fishman. M.J., Gastrfiend, D.R., Miller, M.M
(Eds.). Carson City: The Change Companies.

Beattie, M. 2011. *Codependent No More*. Center City,
MN: Hazeldon

Centers for Disease Control and Prevention. (2014). The public health system and the 10 essential public health services. Retrieved from http://www.cdc.gov/nphpsp/essentialservices

Center for Behavioral Health Statistics and Quality. (2016). Results from the 2015 National Survey on Drug Use and Health: Detailed tables. Rockville, MD: Substance Abuse and Mental Health Services Administration.

Center for Substance Abuse Treatment (CSAT). (2007). *Screening, assessment, and treatment planning for persons with co-occurring disorders*, COCE overview paper 2. Rockville, MD: Substance Abuse and Mental Health Administration, and Center for Mental Health Services (SAMHSA).

Diane Langberg. (2019). Policies. Retrieved from http://www.dianelangberg.com/counseling-practices/policies

Dowell, D., Haegerich, T. M., & R., C. (2016). CDC guideline for prescribing opioids for chronic pain - United States. MMWR, 65(1), 1-49.

National Drug Intelligence Center. (2011). *National drug threat assessment*. Washington, DC: U.S. Department of Justice.

National Institute on Drug Abuse. (2019). Overdose Death Rates. Retrieved from http://www.drugabuse.gov/related-topic/trends-statistics/overdose-death-rates

Pating, D.R., Miller, M.M., Goperlerund, E., Martin, J. & Ziedonis, D. M. (2012). New systems of care for substance use disorders: Treatment, finance, and technology under health care reform. *Psychiatric Clinics of North America 35, 327-356.*

Pennsylvania Department of Drug and Alcohol Programs. (2016). Treatment Manual. http://www.ddap.pa.gov/Manuals/Treatment %20Manual.pdf.

Twelve steps and twelve traditions. (1989). New York, NY: Alcoholics Anonymous World Services.

Trimpey, J.1996. *Rational Recovery*: The New Cure for Substance Addiction. New York: Pocket Books/Simon and Schuster.

U.S. Department of Health and Human Services (HHS), Office of the Surgeon General, *Facing Addiction in America: The Surgeon General's Report on Alcohol, Drugs, and Health.* Washington, DC: HHS, November 2016.

Vaillant, G., Mukamal K. Successful Aging. *American Journal of Psychiatry*, 2001:158:839–847

Volkow, N. D. (2014). America's addiction to opioids: Heroin and prescription drug abuse. Senate Caucus on International Narcotics Control: National Institute on Drug Abuse. Retrieved from https:// www.drugabuse.gov/about-nida/legislative-activities/testimony-to-congress/2015/americasaddiction-to-opioids-heroin-prescription-drug-abuse.

Vox. (2017). *Trump is declaring a national emergency over the opioid epidemic.* Retrieved from https://www.vox.com/platform/amp/policy-and-politics/2017/8/10/16091442/trump-opioid-epidemic-emergency

World Health Organization. (2015). Health systems strengthening glossary, G-H. Health Systems. Retrieved from http://www.who.int/healthsystems/hss_glossary/en/index5.html.

Acknowledgements

Thank you Lefty, for helping me live in gratitude and encouraging me to keep reaching for the stars.

Thank you, Hilary, Zoe, and Judah, for your love and inspiration every day. You make me a better man.

Thank you to my four editors. Editor-in-Chief Jim P, this book does not get completed without your continued help and support. Kathy D, you edited multiple versions of this book and helped me get a solid foundation for this message. Drew, your complete read and edit of this book was no small task, you are a true friend. Kathy C, your time and talents for the final edit will not go unnoticed. All of you have helped make this more enjoyable to read and I know your efforts will help keep this book in the hands of those family systems that are struggling with addiction.

To the countless families, individuals and clients who have allowed me to be a part of their miracle.

Last shall be FIRST. Thank you God for the love and gifts you give me, creating a season in my life so that this book could be published and for continuing to surround me with amazing people. This book is for your children.

Made in the USA
Middletown, DE
21 June 2019